BLOOD TYPE O

RECIPES COOKBOOK

Simple and Delicious, Genetically Tailored

Meals for Your Wellness!

Noreen Hart

Copyright © 2024 by Noreen Hart

Table of Content

Disclaimer

The information provided in this cookbook is intended for educational purposes only and should not be construed as medical advice. The recipes and dietary recommendations are based on general principles and may not be suitable for everyone.

It is recommended to consult with a qualified healthcare professional or dietitian before making any significant changes to your diet, especially if you have any existing medical conditions or dietary restrictions.

The author and publisher are not liable for any consequences resulting from the use or misuse of the information presented in this cookbook.

Introduction

Have you ever felt like you were following all the "rules" for healthy eating, but still didn't feel your best? Embarking on a journey toward better health can be both exhilarating and daunting.

Are you ready to unlock the secret to optimal health and vitality for your blood type?

The 'Blood Type O Recipes Cookbook' is crafted to guide you through the heart of the Blood Type O Diet, offering not just meals, but a transformation in your approach to wellness.

This book is a conversation, a shared meal at the table of knowledge, where every recipe is a whisper of encouragement, telling you that yes, you can enjoy sumptuous food while nurturing your body.

In this cookbook, we'll explore delicious, blood-type O-friendly recipes to help you feel energized, balanced, and vibrantly healthy.

Imagine a world where every bite you take is aligned with your body's needs, where food becomes an ally in your quest for vitality. That's the promise of the Blood Type O Diet, and this cookbook is your roadmap.

But that's not all; we'll also explore the nutritional guidelines and practical tips essential for success on the Blood Type O diet.

Whether you're a seasoned chef or a kitchen novice, you'll find inspiration and guidance to make every meal a celebration of health and flavor.

Get ready to embrace a new way of eating that honors your individuality and empowers you to thrive.

With this cookbook as your companion, you'll discover that eating for your blood type isn't just about following a diet—it's about embracing a lifestyle that promotes vitality, longevity, and joy.

So, are you ready to do this with me? Let's get started and savor the delicious possibilities that await!

Chapter 1

Nutritional Guidelines for Blood Type O

As a Type O, your genetic inheritance traces back to the prehistoric hunters who lived off the land. This means your body is optimally suited for a diet emphasizing lean, protein-rich foods and low in grains, legumes, and dairy.

Focus on High-Quality Protein

Lean meats, poultry, fish, and eggs should make up the staple of your diet as a Type O. Your body has the ability to efficiently metabolize and make use of the high-quality protein and nutrients from animal sources. Opt for grass-fed, organic options when possible.

Limit Grains and Legumes

The hunters of yesteryear consumed very few grains or legumes. As a Type O, your system has a difficult time fully digesting the gluten and lectins found in these foods, which can cause inflammation, digestive issues, and weight gain over time. It's best to avoid or severely limit wheat, rye, corn, beans, lentils, and peanuts.

Load Up on Vegetables

You'll want to fill at least 1⁄3 of your plate with a variety of fresh vegetables at each meal. Beneficial veggies for Type Os include spinach, broccoli, kale, onions, carrots, and peppers. These provide vital nutrients and fiber.

Enjoy Low Sugar Fruits

While type Os should steer clear of very sweet, tropical fruits, berries, plums, grapefruit, and other low-sugar fruits can be enjoyed in moderation as a healthy source of antioxidants.

Healthy Fats are Key

Unlike some diets, the Type O plan encourages consuming healthy fats from olive oil, avocados, coconut oil, nuts, and seeds to promote satiety and brain health. Just make sure you watch your portions.

Stay Hydrated

Drink at least 8 glasses of fresh water daily to support digestion and detoxification. Herbal teas, vegetable juices, and moderate coffee/wine can also be enjoyed.

By prioritizing lean, nutrient-dense protein, fibrous veggies, hydrating fluids, and healthy fats while limiting grains, legumes, and dairy, you'll be aligning your diet with your hunter ancestry for optimal energy, weight control, and overall wellness.

Tips for Success on the Blood Type O Diet

1. **Plan Ahead:** Planning your meals in advance can help you stay on track with your dietary goals. Take some time each week to plan your meals, create a grocery list, and prepare healthy ingredients. Having nutritious options readily available makes it easier to stick to your diet plan.

2. **Focus on Whole Foods:** Emphasize whole, unprocessed foods in your diet, such as lean meats, fish, fruits, vegetables, and nuts. These nutrient-dense foods provide essential vitamins, minerals, and antioxidants that support overall health and well-being.

3. **Read Labels Carefully:** When shopping for packaged foods, read labels carefully to avoid ingredients that may not be compatible with the Blood Type O diet. Look for products free from preservatives, additives, and artificial colors or flavors. Always go for minimally processed options whenever possible.

4. **Stay Hydrated:** Drinking an adequate amount of water is essential for overall health and can help support digestion, metabolism, and energy levels. Aim to drink at least eight glasses of water per day, and consider herbal teas or infused water for added flavor and hydration.

5. **Listen to Your Body:** If you notice any adverse reactions or discomfort after eating

certain foods, consider eliminating them from your diet or reducing your intake. Trusting your body's signals is key to finding the right balance of foods for your individual needs.

6. **Be Mindful of Portions:** While the Blood Type O diet emphasizes nutritious foods, portion control is still important for maintaining a healthy weight and overall well-being. Pay attention to your serving sizes. You should also pay attention to your body's hunger and fullness cues to avoid overeating.

7. **Seek Support:** Joining a community or finding support from friends and family members who are also following the Blood Type O diet can provide encouragement and motivation. Share recipes, meal ideas, and tips for success with others who understand your dietary goals.

8. **Be Flexible:** While it's essential to follow the general guidelines of the Blood Type O diet, it's also important to be flexible and adaptable. Allow yourself the occasional treat or indulgence while staying mindful of your overall

dietary patterns. Strive for consistency rather than perfection.

List of Beneficial and Unsuitable Foods

Beneficial Foods for Blood Type O:

1. **High-Quality Protein:**
   o Lean cuts of beef (preferably grass-fed)
   o Lamb
   o Poultry (chicken, turkey)
   o Game meats (venison, elk)
   o Fish (salmon, mackerel, cod, trout)
   o Shellfish (shrimp, lobster, crab)
   o Eggs
2. **Leafy Greens and Vegetables:**
   o Kale
   o Spinach
   o Broccoli
   o Brussels sprouts
   o Swiss chard
   o Collard greens
   o Sweet potatoes

- Bell peppers
- Onions
- Garlic

3. **Fruits:**
   - Berries (blueberries, strawberries, raspberries)
   - Plums
   - Cherries
   - Prunes
   - Figs
   - Pineapple
   - Papaya

4. **Healthy Fats:**
   - Olive oil
   - Avocado
   - Flaxseed oil
   - Coconut oil
   - Almonds
   - Walnuts

5. **Beans and Legumes (in moderation):**
   - Black beans
   - Adzuki beans

- Lentils
6. **Grains (gluten-free):**
    - Buckwheat
    - Rice (brown or wild)
    - Quinoa
    - Amaranth
7. **Dairy Alternatives:**
    - Almond milk
    - Coconut milk
    - Cashew cheese (in moderation)

Foods to Avoid for Blood Type O:

1. **Dairy Products:**
    - Cow's milk
    - Cheese (except for occasional feta or mozzarella)
    - Yogurt
    - Ice cream
2. **Wheat and Gluten-Containing Foods:**
    - Wheat bread
    - Pasta
    - Cereal

    ◦ Baked goods (cakes, cookies, pastries)

3. **Processed and Refined Foods:**

    ◦ Processed meats (sausage, bacon)

    ◦ Packaged snacks (chips, crackers)

    ◦ Sugary beverages (soda, energy drinks)

    ◦ Artificial sweeteners

4. **Certain Vegetables:**

    ◦ Corn

    ◦ Eggplant

    ◦ Cabbage (limit intake)

5. **Legumes (in excess):**

    ◦ Kidney beans

    ◦ Lima beans

    ◦ Peanuts

6. **Nightshade Vegetables (in moderation):**

    ◦ Tomatoes

    ◦ Potatoes

    ◦ Peppers (bell peppers, chili peppers)

7. **Highly Acidic Fruits (in moderation):**

    ◦ Oranges

    ◦ Strawberries

    ◦ Rhubarb

Kitchen Essentials for Blood Type O Cooking

1. **Quality Chef's Knife:** Invest in a sharp, high-quality chef's knife for slicing, dicing, and chopping vegetables, fruits, and meats with ease.

2. **Cutting Boards:** Have a selection of cutting boards, preferably one for meats and another for fruits and vegetables, to prevent cross-contamination.

3. **Cookware Set:** A versatile cookware set including pots, pans, and skillets made from stainless steel or cast iron for even cooking and durability.

4. **Food Processor or Blender:** Essential for blending sauces, soups, smoothies, and making homemade dressings or marinades.

5. **Measuring Cups and Spoons:** Accurate measurements are crucial for successful cooking and baking, so have a set of measuring cups and spoons on hand.

6. **Mixing Bowls:** Assortment of mixing bowls in various sizes for combining ingredients, marinating meats, and tossing salads.

7. **Baking Sheets and Pans:** Non-stick baking sheets and pans for roasting vegetables, baking homemade bread, and preparing healthy desserts.

8. **Steamer Basket:** Ideal for steaming vegetables while preserving their nutrients and natural flavors.

9. **Grill or Grill Pan:** Great for cooking lean meats, fish, and vegetables with minimal added fat, adding delicious charred flavor.

10. **Herbs and Spices:** Build a collection of herbs and spices to enhance the flavor of your dishes without relying on excessive salt or unhealthy seasonings.

11. **Olive Oil and Vinegar:** Use high-quality olive oil for cooking and drizzling over salads, along with a selection of vinegars for dressings and marinades.

12. **Non-Dairy Milk Alternatives:** Keep non-dairy milk options like almond milk or coconut milk on hand for recipes that call for dairy alternatives.

13. **Storage Containers:** Have a variety of storage containers for storing leftovers, prepped ingredients, and batch-cooked meals in the fridge or freezer.

14. **Sharpie Marker:** Use a marker to label and date your food containers for easy identification and to prevent food waste.

15. **Cookbook or Recipe Binder:** Keep your favorite Blood Type O recipes organized and easily accessible for meal planning and inspiration.

Having these kitchen essentials on hand will help you prepare delicious and nutritious meals that align with the Blood Type O diet, making it easier to maintain a healthy lifestyle.

Chapter 2

Breakfast Recipes for Blood Type O

Kale Salad

- **Preparation Time:** 15 minutes
- **Serves:** 4
- **Size per Serving:** 1 cup

Ingredients:

- 1 bunch of kale, with stems removed and leaves torn into bite-sized pieces
- 1/4 cup extra virgin olive oil
- 2 tablespoons lemon juice
- 1 clove garlic, minced
- 1/4 teaspoon sea salt
- 1/4 teaspoon black pepper
- 1/4 cup grated Parmesan cheese (optional)
- 1/4 cup chopped walnuts (optional)
- 1/4 cup dried cranberries (optional)

Nutritional Information: Calories: 180 | Total Fat: 14g | Carbohydrates: 10g | Fiber: 2g | Protein: 4g

Instructions:

1. In a small bowl, whisk together the olive oil, lemon juice, minced garlic, sea salt, and black pepper to make the dressing.
2. Put the torn kale leaves into a large mixing bowl.
3. Pour the dressing over the kale and use your hands to massage the dressing into the kale leaves for about 2-3 minutes, or until the kale begins to soften and wilt.
4. If desired, add the grated Parmesan cheese, chopped walnuts, and dried cranberries to the salad and toss to combine.
5. Serve the kale salad immediately as a side dish or add protein such as grilled chicken or salmon for a complete meal.

Serving Suggestions: Pair this refreshing kale salad with grilled chicken or salmon for a satisfying and nutritious meal. Alternatively, serve it as a side dish alongside your favorite protein or whole grain for a balanced plate.

Roast Parsnips

- **Preparation Time:** 30 minutes
- **Serves:** 4
- **Size per Serving:** 1/2 cup

Ingredients:

- 4 parsnips, peeled and cut into 1-inch pieces
- 2 tablespoons olive oil
- 1 teaspoon dried thyme
- 1 teaspoon garlic powder
- Sea salt and black pepper to taste

Nutritional Information: Calories: 120 | Total Fat: 7g | Carbohydrates: 15g | Fiber: 5g | Protein: 1g

Instructions:

1. Preheat your oven to 400°F (200°C).
2. In a large bowl, toss the parsnip pieces with olive oil, dried thyme, garlic powder, sea salt, and black pepper until evenly coated.
3. Spread the seasoned parsnips in a single layer on a baking sheet lined with parchment paper or aluminum foil.
4. Roast the parsnips in the preheated oven for 25-30 minutes, or until they are tender and

golden brown, flipping them halfway through the cooking time for even browning.

5. Remove the roasted parsnips from the oven and transfer them to a serving dish.

6. Serve the roast parsnips as a delicious side dish alongside your favorite protein or incorporate them into salads or grain bowls for added flavor and texture.

Serving Suggestions: Enjoy these flavorful roast parsnips as a nutritious side dish to complement any meal. Pair them with roasted chicken or grilled fish for a complete and satisfying dinner. Alternatively, add them to salads or grain bowls for a tasty and wholesome lunch option.

Omelet with Diced Lamb and Bell Peppers

- **Preparation Time:** 15 minutes
- **Serves:** 2
- **Size per Serving:** 1 omelet

Ingredients:

- 4 large eggs
- 1/2 cup diced cooked lamb

- 1/2 cup diced bell peppers (any color)
- 1 tablespoon olive oil
- Salt and black pepper to taste
- Fresh herbs for garnish (optional)

Nutritional Information: Calories: 280 | Total Fat: 20g | Carbohydrates: 3g | Fiber: 1g | Protein: 22g

Instructions:

1. In a bowl, whisk the eggs until they are thoroughly combined. Season with black pepper and salt according to your palate.
2. Set a non-stick pan on medium and let the olive oil heat gently.
3. Add the diced lamb and bell peppers to the skillet and cook for 3-4 minutes, or until the bell peppers are tender.
4. Pour the beaten eggs over the lamb and bell peppers in the skillet, spreading them evenly.
5. Cook the omelet for 3-4 minutes, or until the edges are set and the bottom is golden brown.
6. Using a spatula, gently fold the omelet in half and continue cooking for another 1-2 minutes, or until the eggs are cooked through.

7. Transfer the omelet onto a serving plate and, if desired, garnish with fresh herbs.

8. Serve the omelet hot as a nutritious and protein-packed breakfast or brunch option.

Serving Suggestions: Enjoy this delicious omelet with diced lamb and bell peppers alongside whole grain toast or a side salad for a balanced meal. You can also customize the omelet by adding other vegetables or herbs according to your preference.

Sardine Patties

- **Preparation Time:** 20 minutes
- **Serves:** 4
- **Size per Serving:** 2 patties

Ingredients:

- 2 cans (4.4 ounces each) of sardines in olive oil, drained
- 1/4 cup almond flour
- 1/4 cup finely chopped onion
- 1/4 cup finely chopped parsley
- 1 egg, beaten
- 1 tablespoon lemon juice
- 1 teaspoon Dijon mustard

- Salt and black pepper to taste
- 2 tablespoons olive oil (for frying)

Nutritional Information: Calories: 180 | Total Fat: 12g | Carbohydrates: 4g | Fiber: 1g | Protein: 14g

Instructions:

1. In a large mixing bowl, mash the drained sardines with a fork until they are broken down into small pieces.

2. Add almond flour, chopped onion, chopped parsley, beaten egg, lemon juice, Dijon mustard, salt, and black pepper to the bowl with the mashed sardines. Mix until well combined.

3. Form the mixture into small patties, about 2 inches in diameter.

4. Heat olive oil in your skillet on medium heat.

5. Once the oil is hot, carefully add the sardine patties to the skillet in a single layer, making sure not to overcrowd the pan.

6. Cook your patties for 3-5 minutes on each side, or until they turn golden brown and crispy.

7. Once cooked through, remove the patties from the skillet and place them on a plate lined with paper towels to drain any excess oil.

8. Serve the sardine patties hot as a protein-rich appetizer or main dish. They can also be enjoyed cold as a nutritious snack or added to salads for extra flavor and protein.

Serving Suggestions: Serve these crispy sardine patties with a side of fresh lemon wedges and your favorite dipping sauce, such as tartar sauce or aioli. Pair them with a green salad or steamed vegetables for a complete and satisfying meal.

Buckwheat Scandinavian Pancakes

- **Preparation Time:** 20 minutes
- **Serves:** 4
- **Size per Serving:** 3 pancakes

Ingredients:

- 1 cup buckwheat flour
- 1 tablespoon coconut sugar (optional)
- 1 teaspoon baking powder
- 1/4 teaspoon salt
- 2 large eggs

- 1 cup of almond milk (or any non-dairy milk you like)
- 1 tablespoon coconut oil, melted
- Fresh berries and maple syrup for serving (optional)

Nutritional Information: Calories: 190 | Total Fat: 6g | Carbohydrates: 27g | Fiber: 4g | Protein: 7g

Instructions:

1. In a large mixing bowl, whisk together the buckwheat flour, coconut sugar (if using), baking powder, and salt until well combined.

2. In a separate bowl, beat the eggs, then add almond milk and melted coconut oil, and whisk until smooth.

3. Combine the wet ingredients with the dry ingredients and stir until they are just mixed together. Be cautious not to overmix; it's fine if there are a few lumps in the batter.

4. Warm a non-stick skillet or griddle over medium heat and lightly grease it with coconut oil or cooking spray.

5. Pour approximately 1/4 cup of batter onto the skillet for each pancake.

6. Cook the pancakes for 2-3 minutes on one side, or until bubbles form on the surface and the edges begin to set.

7. Flip the pancakes and continue cooking for an extra 1-2 minutes on the other side, or until they are golden brown and thoroughly cooked.

8. Repeat the process with the remaining batter, adjusting the heat as necessary to prevent burning.

9. Serve the buckwheat pancakes warm with fresh berries and a drizzle of maple syrup, if desired.

Serving Suggestions: Enjoy these wholesome buckwheat Scandinavian pancakes for breakfast or brunch topped with your favorite fruits, nuts, or seeds for added flavor and texture. Pair them with a side of Greek yogurt or a smoothie for a complete and satisfying meal.

Poached Eggs & Sweet Potatoes

- **Preparation Time:** 30 minutes
- **Serves:** 2
- **Size per Serving:** 1 poached egg with sweet potatoes

Ingredients:

- 2 large sweet potatoes, peeled and sliced into rounds
- 4 large eggs
- 1 tablespoon white vinegar
- Salt and black pepper to taste
- Fresh parsley or chives for garnish (optional)

Nutritional Information: Calories: 220 | Total Fat: 8g | Carbohydrates: 30g | Fiber: 5g | Protein: 10g

Instructions:

1. Fill a large pot with water and heat it until it reaches a gentle simmer over medium heat.
2. Carefully add the sweet potato rounds to the simmering water and cook for 10-15 minutes, or until they are tender but still hold their shape.

3. While the sweet potatoes are cooking, crack each egg into a small bowl or ramekin.

4. Add the white vinegar to the simmering water and use a spoon to create a gentle whirlpool in the center of the pot.

5. Slowly pour the eggs, one at a time, into the center of the whirlpool. Cook for 3-4 minutes, or until the egg whites are fully set but the yolks remain runny.

6. Use a slotted spoon to carefully remove the poached eggs from the water and transfer them to a plate lined with paper towels to drain any excess water.

7. Drain the cooked sweet potatoes and arrange them on serving plates.

8. Place a poached egg on top of each serving of sweet potatoes.

9. Season with salt and black pepper to taste, and garnish with fresh parsley or chives if desired.

10. Serve the poached eggs and sweet potatoes hot as a nutritious and satisfying breakfast or brunch option.

Serving Suggestions: Enjoy this simple and wholesome dish on its own or pair it with a side salad or steamed vegetables for added nutrition. Sprinkle with your favorite herbs or spices for extra flavor, and serve with whole grain toast or avocado slices for a complete and balanced meal.

Easy Salmon Pesto

- **Preparation Time:** 20 minutes
- **Serves:** 2
- **Size per Serving:** 1 filet with pesto

Ingredients:

- 2 salmon filets (about 6 ounces each)
- 2 tablespoons prepared pesto
- 1 tablespoon olive oil
- Salt and black pepper to taste
- Lemon wedges for serving

Nutritional Information: Calories: 350 | Total Fat: 24g | Carbohydrates: 1g | Fiber: 0g | Protein: 32g

Instructions:

1. Preheat your oven to 400°F (200°C).
2. Place the salmon filets on a baking sheet lined with parchment paper or aluminum foil.
3. Season the salmon filets with salt and black pepper to taste.
4. Spread 1 tablespoon of prepared pesto evenly over each salmon filet.
5. Drizzle olive oil over the top of the pesto-coated salmon filets.
6. Bake the salmon in the preheated oven for 12-15 minutes, or until the fish is cooked through and flakes easily with a fork.
7. Take the salmon out of the oven and allow it to rest for a few minutes before serving.
8. Serve the easy salmon pesto hot with lemon wedges on the side for squeezing over the fish.

Serving Suggestions: Enjoy this salmon pesto dish with a side of steamed vegetables or a green salad for a complete and balanced meal. Pair it with quinoa, brown rice, or roasted potatoes for added fiber and complex carbohydrates.

Lunch Recipes for Blood Type O
Spinach Feta Rice

- **Preparation Time:** 25 minutes
- **Serves:** 4
- **Size per Serving:** 1 cup

Ingredients:

- 1 cup long-grain brown rice
- 2 cups vegetable broth
- 2 cups fresh spinach leaves, chopped
- 1/2 cup crumbled feta cheese
- 2 tablespoons olive oil
- 2 cloves garlic, minced
- Salt and black pepper to taste

Nutritional Information: Calories: 220 | Total Fat: 9g | Carbohydrates: 30g | Fiber: 3g | Protein: 6g

Instructions:

1. Rinse your brown rice under cold water until the water runs clear. Drain well.
2. In a medium saucepan, combine the rinsed rice and vegetable broth. Bring the mixture to a boil over high heat.

3. Reduce the heat to low, cover, and simmer for 20-25 minutes, or until the rice is tender and all the liquid is absorbed.
4. In a large skillet, heat olive oil over medium heat. Add minced garlic to the skillet and cook for 1-2 minutes, or until it becomes fragrant.
5. Add chopped spinach to the skillet and cook until wilted, about 2-3 minutes.
6. Once the rice is cooked, fluff it with a fork and transfer it to the skillet with the spinach.
7. Add crumbled feta cheese to the skillet and gently toss everything together until well combined.
8. Season with black pepper and salt according to your palate.
9. Serve the spinach feta rice hot as a delicious and nutritious lunch option or as a side dish to your favorite protein.

Serving Suggestions: Enjoy this flavorful spinach feta rice on its own or pair it with grilled chicken or roasted vegetables for a balanced and satisfying meal.

Rose Sauce with Pasta

- **Preparation Time:** 30 minutes
- **Serves:** 4
- **Size per Serving:** 1 cup of pasta with sauce

Ingredients:

- 8 ounces gluten-free pasta (such as brown rice or quinoa pasta)
- 2 tablespoons olive oil
- 2 cloves garlic, minced
- 1/2 onion, finely chopped
- 1 can (14 ounces) crushed tomatoes
- 1/2 cup unsweetened almond milk
- 1/4 cup tomato paste
- 1 teaspoon dried basil
- 1 teaspoon dried oregano
- Salt and black pepper to taste
- Fresh basil leaves for garnish (optional)

Nutritional Information: Calories: 250 | Total Fat: 7g | Carbohydrates: 40g | Fiber: 5g | Protein: 5g

Instructions:

1. Prepare the gluten-free pasta according to the package instructions, cooking until it reaches an al dente texture.
2. Drain and set aside.
3. In a large skillet, heat olive oil over medium heat. Add minced garlic and chopped onion, and sauté for 2-3 minutes, or until fragrant and softened.
4. Stir in the crushed tomatoes, almond milk, tomato paste, dried basil, and dried oregano. Season with black pepper and salt according to your palate.
5. Simmer the sauce for 10-15 minutes, stirring occasionally, until it thickens slightly and the flavors meld together.
6. Once the sauce is ready, add the cooked pasta to the skillet and toss to coat evenly with the sauce.
7. Cook for an additional 2-3 minutes, or until the pasta is heated through.
8. Serve the rose sauce pasta hot, garnished with fresh basil leaves if desired.

Serving Suggestions: Enjoy this creamy and flavorful rose sauce pasta on its own or with a side of steamed vegetables for a complete and satisfying meal. Sprinkle with nutritional yeast or grated Parmesan cheese for added flavor, if desired.

Tofu with Sauteed Vegetables

- **Preparation Time:** 25 minutes
- **Serves:** 4
- **Size per Serving:** 1 cup of tofu with vegetables

Ingredients:

- 14 ounces firm tofu, drained and pressed
- 2 tablespoons tamari or soy sauce
- 2 tablespoons olive oil
- 2 cloves garlic, minced
- 1 bell pepper, thinly sliced
- 1 zucchini, thinly sliced
- 1 cup sliced mushrooms
- 2 cups spinach leaves
- 1 tablespoon sesame seeds (optional)
- Salt and black pepper to taste
- Red pepper flakes for garnish (optional)

Nutritional Information: Calories: 200 | Total Fat: 12g | Carbohydrates: 10g | Fiber: 3g | Protein: 16g

Instructions:

1. Cut the pressed tofu into cubes and place them in a bowl. Drizzle with tamari or soy sauce and toss to coat evenly. Allow the mixture to marinate for 10-15 minutes.

2. Warm olive oil in a skillet on medium heat. Add minced garlic to the skillet and sauté for about 1 minute, or until it becomes fragrant.

3. Add sliced bell pepper, zucchini, and mushrooms to the skillet. Cook for 5-8 minutes, or until you have tender vegetables.

4. Push the vegetables to one side of the skillet and add the marinated tofu cubes to the empty side. Cook for 3-5 mins on each side, or until it turns golden brown and crispy.

5. Once the tofu is cooked through, add spinach leaves to the skillet and cook for 1-2 minutes, or until wilted.

6. Season the tofu and vegetables with salt, black pepper, and sesame seeds (if using). Toss everything together until well combined.
7. Top with red pepper flakes for a dash of spice, if desired.
8. Serve the tofu with sautéed vegetables hot as a nutritious and satisfying lunch or dinner option.

Serving Suggestions: Enjoy this flavorful tofu with sautéed vegetables on its own or with a side of quinoa or brown rice for added protein and fiber. Drizzle with additional tamari or soy sauce for extra flavor, if desired.

Vegetarian Lasagna

- **Preparation Time:** 1 hour
- **Serves:** 6
- **Size per Serving:** 1 slice

Ingredients:
- 9 lasagna noodles (gluten-free if preferred)
- 2 cups marinara sauce
- 1 cup ricotta cheese (or tofu ricotta for vegan option)

- 1 cup shredded mozzarella cheese (or dairy-free alternative)
- 1 cup chopped spinach
- 1 cup sliced mushrooms
- 1/2 cup grated of Parmesan cheese (or any dairy-free alternative)
- 2 cloves garlic, minced
- 1 tablespoon olive oil
- Salt and black pepper to taste
- Fresh basil leaves for garnish (optional)

Nutritional Information: Calories: 350 | Total Fat: 15g | Carbohydrates: 35g | Fiber: 4g | Protein: 18g

Instructions:

1. Preheat your oven to 375°F (190°C). Grease your 9x13-inch baking dish with olive oil.
2. Follow the package instructions to cook the lasagna noodles until al dente. Drain and set aside.
3. In a large skillet, heat olive oil over medium heat. Add minced garlic to the skillet and sauté for about 1 minute, or until it becomes fragrant.

4. Add sliced mushrooms to the skillet and cook for 5-7 minutes, or until they release their moisture and become tender. Season with black pepper and salt according to your palate.

5. In a bowl, mix together ricotta cheese (or tofu ricotta), chopped spinach, and sautéed mushrooms until well combined.

6. Spread a thin layer of marinara sauce evenly on the bottom of the baking dish.

7. Place three lasagna noodles on top of the marinara sauce.

8. Spread half of the ricotta cheese mixture over the noodles, followed by a layer of marinara sauce and shredded mozzarella cheese.

9. Repeat the layers with the remaining noodles, ricotta cheese mixture, marinara sauce, and mozzarella cheese.

10. Sprinkle grated Parmesan cheese over the top layer of mozzarella cheese.

11. Cover the baking dish with aluminum foil and place it in the preheated oven to bake for 30 minutes.

12. Remove the foil and bake for an additional 15 minutes, or until the cheese is melted and bubbly.

13. Let the vegetarian lasagna cool for a few minutes before slicing.

14. If desired, garnish with fresh basil leaves before serving.

Serving Suggestions: Serve this hearty vegetarian lasagna with a side salad and garlic bread for a comforting and satisfying meal. You can also customize the lasagna by adding your favorite vegetables or herbs to the ricotta cheese mixture for extra flavor and nutrition.

Curried Shrimp

- **Preparation Time:** 20 minutes
- **Serves:** 4
- **Size per Serving:** 1 cup

Ingredients:

- 1 pound shrimp, peeled and deveined
- 1 tablespoon olive oil
- 1 onion, diced
- 2 cloves garlic, minced

- 1 tablespoon curry powder
- 1 teaspoon ground turmeric
- 1/2 teaspoon ground cumin
- 1/2 teaspoon ground coriander
- 1/4 teaspoon of cayenne pepper (not compulsory; for extra heat)
- 1 cup coconut milk
- 1 cup diced tomatoes (canned or fresh)
- Salt and black pepper to taste
- Fresh cilantro for garnish (optional)

Nutritional Information: Calories: 220 | Total Fat: 11g | Carbohydrates: 7g | Fiber: 2g | Protein: 23g

Instructions:

1. Warm olive oil in a skillet on medium heat. Add diced onion and minced garlic, and sauté for 2-3 minutes, or until softened and fragrant.

2. Add curry powder, ground turmeric, ground cumin, ground coriander, and cayenne pepper (if using) to the skillet. Stir to coat the onions and garlic in the spices.

3. Add your peeled and deveined shrimp to the skillet. Cook for 2-3 minutes, or until the shrimp turn pink and opaque.
4. Pour in the coconut milk and diced tomatoes. Stir to combine all the ingredients.
5. Simmer the curry shrimp mixture for 5-7 minutes, or until the sauce thickens slightly and the flavors meld together.
6. Season with black pepper and salt according to your palate.
7. Garnish with fresh cilantro before serving, if desired.
8. Serve the curried shrimp hot over cooked rice or quinoa, or alongside steamed vegetables for a complete and satisfying meal.

Serving Suggestions: Enjoy this flavorful curried shrimp dish with your choice of rice or quinoa for a balanced and nutritious lunch or dinner. You can also serve it with naan bread or roti for a traditional Indian-inspired meal. Adjust the level of spice according to your preference by adding more or less cayenne pepper.

Lemon-herb roasted Chicken with Green Beans

- **Preparation Time:** 1 hour
- **Serves:** 4
- **Size per Serving:** 1 chicken breast with green beans

Ingredients:

- 4 boneless, skinless chicken breasts
- 2 tablespoons olive oil
- 2 cloves garlic, minced
- 1 tablespoon lemon zest
- 2 tablespoons lemon juice
- 1 teaspoon dried thyme
- 1 teaspoon dried rosemary
- 1 teaspoon dried oregano
- 1/2 teaspoon paprika
- Salt and black pepper to taste
- 1 pound green beans, trimmed
- Lemon wedges for serving

Nutritional Information: Calories: 280 | Total Fat: 10g | Carbohydrates: 9g | Fiber: 4g | Protein: 38g

Instructions:

1. Preheat your oven to 400°F (200°C). Grease a baking dish with olive oil or line it with parchment paper.

2. In a small bowl, whisk together olive oil, minced garlic, lemon zest, lemon juice, dried thyme, dried rosemary, dried oregano, paprika, salt, and black pepper to make the marinade.

3. Place the chicken breasts in the prepared baking dish and pour the marinade over them, making sure they are evenly coated.

4. Arrange the trimmed green beans around the chicken breasts in the baking dish. Sprinkle a little olive oil and season with black pepper and salt

5. Place the baking dish in the preheated oven and roast for 25-30 minutes, or until the chicken is cooked through and the green beans are tender.

6. Once done, take the baking dish out of the oven and allow it to rest for a few minutes.

7. Serve the lemon-herb roasted chicken with green beans hot, garnished with lemon wedges for squeezing over the chicken.

Serving Suggestions: Enjoy this delicious lemon-herb roasted chicken with green beans as a wholesome and satisfying meal. Pair it with a side of quinoa, brown rice, or roasted potatoes for added fiber and carbohydrates. Sprinkle with fresh chopped parsley or basil for extra flavor and freshness.

Gluten-Free Oven-Fried Cod

- **Preparation Time:** 25 minutes
- **Serves:** 4
- **Size per Serving:** 1 filet

Ingredients:

- 4 cod filets (about 6 ounces each)
- 1/2 cup gluten-free breadcrumbs
- 1/4 cup almond flour
- 1 teaspoon paprika
- 1/2 teaspoon garlic powder
- 1/2 teaspoon onion powder
- 1/4 teaspoon dried thyme
- Salt and black pepper to taste

- 2 eggs, beaten
- Olive oil spray

Nutritional Information: Calories: 250 | Total Fat: 8g | Carbohydrates: 8g | Fiber: 1g | Protein: 36g

Instructions:

1. Preheat your oven to 425°F (220°C). Line a baking sheet with parchment paper or aluminum foil and lightly grease with olive oil spray.
2. In a shallow dish, combine gluten-free breadcrumbs, almond flour, paprika, garlic powder, onion powder, dried thyme, salt, and black pepper. Mix well to combine.
3. In another shallow dish, place beaten eggs.
4. Dip each cod filet into the beaten eggs, ensuring it is fully coated.
5. Then dredge the cod filet in the breadcrumb mixture, pressing gently to adhere the breadcrumbs to the fish.
6. Arrange the coated cod filets on the prepared baking sheet.

7. Lightly spray the tops of the coated cod filets with olive oil spray.

8. Bake in the preheated oven for 12-15 minutes, or until the cod is cooked through and the coating is golden brown and crispy.

9. Once cooked, remove the cod filets from the oven and let them cool for a few minutes before serving.

10. Serve the gluten-free oven-fried cod hot with lemon wedges and your favorite dipping sauce, such as tartar sauce or aioli.

Serving Suggestions: Enjoy this crispy and flavorful gluten-free oven-fried cod as a delicious and healthy alternative to traditional fried fish. Serve it with a side of steamed vegetables or a fresh green salad for a balanced and nutritious meal. Alternatively, use the cod filets to make fish tacos by wrapping them in corn tortillas and topping with salsa, avocado, and shredded cabbage.

Dinner Recipes for Blood Type O

Black Bean Soup with Meat

- **Preparation Time:** 1 hour
- **Serves:** 6
- **Size per Serving:** 1 cup

Ingredients:

- 2 tablespoons olive oil
- 1 onion, diced
- 2 cloves garlic, minced
- 1 pound ground beef or turkey
- 2 cans (15 ounces each) black beans, drained and rinsed
- 1 can (14.5 ounces) diced tomatoes
- 4 cups beef or vegetable broth
- 1 teaspoon ground cumin
- 1 teaspoon chili powder
- Salt and black pepper to taste
- Fresh cilantro for garnish (optional)
- Greek yogurt for serving or Sour cream (optional)

Nutritional Information: Calories: 300 | Total Fat: 10g | Carbohydrates: 30g | Fiber: 10g | Protein: 20g

Instructions:

1. Heat olive oil in a pot on medium heat. Add diced onion and minced garlic, and sauté for 2-3 minutes until softened and fragrant.

2. Add ground beef or turkey to the pot and cook until browned, breaking it up with a spoon as it cooks.

3. Once the meat is cooked, add drained black beans, diced tomatoes, beef or vegetable broth, ground cumin, and chili powder to the pot. Stir to combine.

4. Bring the soup to a simmer, then reduce the heat to low and let it simmer for 30-40 minutes, stirring occasionally, to allow the flavors to meld together and the soup to thicken slightly.

5. Season the black bean soup with salt and black pepper to taste.

6. Ladle the soup into bowls and garnish with fresh cilantro if desired. Serve hot with a dollop of sour cream or Greek yogurt on top, if desired.

Serving Suggestions: Enjoy this hearty black bean soup with meat on its own or with a side of crusty bread or tortilla chips for dipping. You can also customize the soup by adding your favorite toppings such as shredded cheese, diced avocado, or sliced jalapeños for extra flavor and texture.

Chicken Veggie Soup

- **Preparation Time:** 45 minutes
- **Serves:** 6
- **Size per Serving:** 1 cup

Ingredients:

- 1 tablespoon olive oil
- 1 onion, diced
- 2 carrots, diced
- 2 celery stalks, diced
- 2 cloves garlic, minced
- 1 pound boneless, skinless chicken breasts, diced
- 6 cups chicken broth
- 1 can (14.5 ounces) diced tomatoes
- 1 cup chopped green beans
- 1 cup corn kernels (fresh or frozen)

- 1 teaspoon dried thyme
- 1 teaspoon dried rosemary
- Salt and black pepper to taste
- Fresh parsley for garnish (optional)

Nutritional Information: Calories: 180 | Total Fat: 4g | Carbohydrates: 14g | Fiber: 3g | Protein: 20g

Instructions:

1. Heat olive oil in a pot on medium heat. Add diced onion, carrots, and celery, and sauté for 5-7 minutes until softened.
2. Add your minced garlic to the pot and sauté for an extra 1-3 minutes until fragrant.
3. Add diced chicken breasts to the pot and cook until browned on all sides.
4. Pour in chicken broth and diced tomatoes, and bring the soup to a simmer.
5. Add chopped green beans, corn kernels, dried thyme, and dried rosemary to the pot. Stir to combine.
6. Season the soup with salt and black pepper to taste.

7. Let the soup simmer for 20-25 minutes, stirring occasionally, until the vegetables are tender and the chicken is cooked through.
8. Taste and adjust seasoning if necessary.
9. Ladle the chicken veggie soup into bowls and garnish with fresh parsley if desired.
10. Serve hot as a comforting and nutritious dinner option.

Serving Suggestions: Enjoy this wholesome chicken veggie soup on its own or with a side of crusty bread or crackers for dipping. You can also add cooked rice or pasta to the soup for a heartier meal, or top it with grated Parmesan cheese for extra flavor.

Gluten-Free Pizza Crust

- **Preparation Time:** 1 hour 30 minutes
- **Serves:** 4 (2 10-inch pizzas)
- **Size per Serving:** 1/2 pizza crust

Ingredients:

- 2 cups gluten-free all-purpose flour
- 1 teaspoon xanthan gum
- 1 teaspoon baking powder
- 1/2 teaspoon salt

- 1 tablespoon active dry yeast
- 1 tablespoon honey or maple syrup
- 1 cup warm water (110°F/45°C)
- 2 tablespoons olive oil
- 1 teaspoon apple cider vinegar

Nutritional Information: (per 1/2 pizza crust) Calories: 230 | Total Fat: 6g | Carbohydrates: 40g | Fiber: 3g | Protein: 3g

Instructions:

1. In a large mixing bowl, combine gluten-free all-purpose flour, xanthan gum, baking powder, and salt. Mix well and set aside.

2. In a small bowl, dissolve active dry yeast and honey (or maple syrup) in warm water. Let it sit for 5-10 minutes until frothy.

3. Add olive oil and apple cider vinegar to the yeast mixture and stir to combine.

4. Pour your wet ingredients into your dry ingredients and mix until you have a dough.

5. Knead the dough on a lightly floured surface for 3-5 minutes until smooth and elastic.

6. Divide the dough into two equal portions and form each portion into a ball.

7. Place the dough balls on a parchment-lined baking sheet and cover with a clean kitchen towel. Allow them to rise in a warm place for 1 hour.

8. Preheat your oven to 425°F (220°C).

9. After the dough has risen, place one dough ball on a piece of parchment paper and use your hands to flatten and shape it into a 10-inch circle (or desired pizza shape). Repeat with the second dough ball.

10. Par-bake the pizza crusts in the preheated oven for 8-10 minutes, or until they are set and slightly golden.

11. Remove the par-baked crusts from the oven and add your favorite toppings.

12. Return the pizzas to the oven and bake for an additional 10-12 minutes, or until the crusts are golden brown and crispy and the toppings are heated through.

13. Slice and serve hot.

Serving Suggestions: Customize your gluten-free pizza crust with your favorite toppings such as tomato sauce, cheese, vegetables, and protein options like chicken or tofu. Enjoy it as a delicious and satisfying dinner option for the whole family.

Chinese Stir-Fry

- **Preparation Time:** 30 minutes
- **Serves:** 4
- **Size per Serving:** 1 cup

Ingredients:

- 1 tablespoon sesame oil
- 2 tablespoons of soy sauce (or use tamari for gluten-free option)
- 1 tablespoon rice vinegar
- 1 tablespoon honey or maple syrup
- 1 teaspoon cornstarch
- 2 tablespoons vegetable oil
- 1 pound chicken breast or tofu, cut into bite-sized pieces
- 2 cloves garlic, minced
- 1 tablespoon ginger, minced
- 1 bell pepper, sliced

- 1 cup broccoli florets
- 1 cup sliced carrots
- 1 cup snow peas
- Cooked rice or noodles for serving

Nutritional Information: (per serving) Calories: 250 | Total Fat: 10g | Carbohydrates: 20g | Fiber: 5g | Protein: 20g

Instructions:

1. In a small bowl, whisk together sesame oil, soy sauce, rice vinegar, honey (or maple syrup), and cornstarch to make the sauce. Set aside.
2. Heat vegetable oil in a skillet or wok on medium-high heat.
3. Add minced garlic and minced ginger to the skillet and sauté for 1 minute until fragrant.
4. Add chicken breast or tofu to the skillet and cook until browned and cooked through.
5. Add sliced bell pepper, broccoli florets, sliced carrots, and snow peas to the skillet. Stir-fry for 3-4 minutes until the vegetables are tender-crisp.

6. Pour the prepared sauce over the chicken or tofu and vegetables in the skillet. Stir well to coat everything evenly.

7. Cook for an additional 2-3 minutes until the sauce thickens slightly and coats the stir-fry ingredients.

8. Remove from heat and serve the Chinese stir-fry hot over cooked rice or noodles.

Serving Suggestions: Enjoy this flavorful Chinese stir-fry with your choice of rice or noodles for a satisfying and wholesome dinner. Garnish with sliced green onions, sesame seeds, or crushed red pepper flakes for extra flavor and presentation. Customize the stir-fry by adding your favorite vegetables or protein options such as shrimp or beef.

Fried Oyster Mushroom Mash

- **Preparation Time:** 30 minutes
- **Serves:** 4
- **Size per Serving:** 1 cup

Ingredients:

- 1 pound oyster mushrooms, cleaned and sliced
- 2 tablespoons olive oil

- 2 cloves garlic, minced
- 1 onion, finely chopped
- 1/2 teaspoon smoked paprika
- Salt and black pepper to taste
- Chopped fresh parsley for garnish (optional)

Nutritional Information: (per serving) Calories: 120 | Total Fat: 7g | Carbohydrates: 12g | Fiber: 3g | Protein: 5g

Instructions:

1. Warm olive oil in a skillet on medium heat. Add minced garlic and chopped onion, and sauté for 2-3 minutes until softened.
2. Add sliced oyster mushrooms to the skillet and cook for 5-7 minutes until they release their moisture and become golden brown and crispy.
3. Season the mushrooms with smoked paprika, salt, and black pepper to taste. Stir to combine.
4. Continue cooking for another 2-3 minutes, stirring occasionally, until the mushrooms are well-cooked and crispy.

5. Once cooked, remove the skillet from heat and transfer the fried oyster mushrooms to a serving dish.

6. Garnish with chopped fresh parsley if desired.

7. Serve the fried oyster mushroom mash hot as a flavorful and nutritious side dish or as a topping for salads, sandwiches, or grain bowls.

Serving Suggestions: Enjoy this crispy and savory fried oyster mushroom mash as a tasty alternative to traditional mashed potatoes. Serve it alongside your favorite protein such as grilled chicken, fish, or tofu for a complete and satisfying meal. You can also use it as a filling for wraps or tacos for a delicious plant-based option.

Quick Bean Casserole

- **Preparation Time:** 35 minutes
- **Serves:** 6
- **Size per Serving:** 1 cup

Ingredients:

- 2 cans (15 ounces each) beans (black beans, kidney beans, or a mix), drained and rinsed
- 1 onion, diced

- 2 cloves garlic, minced
- 1 bell pepper, diced
- 1 cup corn kernels (fresh or frozen)
- 1 can (14.5 ounces) diced tomatoes
- 1 teaspoon chili powder
- 1/2 teaspoon cumin
- Salt and black pepper to taste
- 1 cup of shredded cheese (mozzarella or cheddar), optional
- Fresh cilantro for garnish (optional)

Nutritional Information: (per serving, without cheese) Calories: 200 | Total Fat: 2g | Carbohydrates: 35g | Fiber: 10g | Protein: 12g

Instructions:

1. Preheat your oven to 375°F (190°C).
2. In a large skillet, heat olive oil over medium heat. Add diced onion and cook until softened, about 3-4 minutes.
3. Add minced garlic and diced bell pepper to the skillet. Cook for another 2-3 minutes until the vegetables are tender.

4. Add drained and rinsed beans, corn kernels, diced tomatoes, chili powder, cumin, salt, and black pepper to the skillet. Stir to combine.

5. Cook the bean mixture for 5-7 minutes, stirring occasionally, until heated through and flavors meld together.

6. Transfer the bean mixture to a greased baking dish.

7. If using shredded cheese, sprinkle it evenly over the top of the bean mixture.

8. Bake in the preheated oven for 20-25 minutes, or until the casserole is bubbly and the cheese is melted and golden brown.

9. Take out of the oven and allow it to cool for a few minutes before serving.

10. Garnish with fresh cilantro if desired.

11. Serve the quick bean casserole hot as a hearty and nutritious dinner option.

Serving Suggestions: Enjoy this flavorful quick bean casserole on its own or with a side of cooked rice, quinoa, or crusty bread for a complete and satisfying meal. You can also top it with avocado slices, salsa, or Greek yogurt for added flavor and creaminess.

Creamy Tuna Broccoli Rice

- **Preparation Time:** 30 minutes
- **Serves:** 4
- **Size per Serving:** 1 cup

Ingredients:

- 1 cup long-grain white rice
- 2 cups water or chicken broth
- 1 tablespoon olive oil
- 1 onion, diced
- 2 cloves garlic, minced
- 2 cups broccoli florets
- 2 cans (5 ounces each) tuna, drained
- 1/2 cup plain Greek yogurt
- 1/4 cup grated Parmesan cheese
- Salt and black pepper to taste
- Chopped fresh parsley for garnish (optional)

Nutritional Information: (per serving) Calories: 300 | Total Fat: 7g | Carbohydrates: 35g | Fiber: 3g | Protein: 25g

Instructions:

1. Rinse the rice under cold water until the water runs clear. Drain well.

2. In a saucepan, bring water or chicken broth to a boil. Add the rinsed rice, reduce the heat to low, cover, and simmer for 18-20 minutes, or until the rice is tender and the liquid is absorbed.

3. In a large skillet, heat olive oil over medium heat. Add diced onion and minced garlic, and sauté for 2-3 minutes until softened and fragrant.

4. Add broccoli florets to the skillet and cook for 4-5 minutes until tender-crisp.

5. Add drained tuna to the skillet and stir to combine with the onion and broccoli mixture.

6. Stir in cooked rice, plain Greek yogurt, and grated Parmesan cheese. Mix well until everything is evenly coated and heated through.

7. Season with black pepper and salt according to your palate.

8. Garnish with chopped fresh parsley if desired.

9. Serve the creamy tuna broccoli rice hot as a comforting and nutritious dinner option.

Serving Suggestions: Enjoy this creamy tuna broccoli rice dish on its own or with a side salad for a balanced and satisfying meal. You can also customize the dish by adding other vegetables such as bell peppers, peas, or spinach for extra flavor and nutrition.

Desserts/Snacks for Blood Type O
Ginger Chocolate Pound Cake

- **Preparation Time:** 1 hour 30 minutes
- **Serves:** 8
- **Size per Serving:** 1 slice

Ingredients:

- 1 1/2 cups almond flour
- 1/2 cup unsweetened cocoa powder
- 1 teaspoon baking powder
- 1/2 teaspoon baking soda
- 1/4 teaspoon salt
- 1/2 cup honey or maple syrup

- 1/4 cup melted coconut oil
- 3 large eggs
- 1/4 cup plain Greek yogurt
- 2 teaspoons vanilla extract
- 2 teaspoons ground ginger
- 1/2 cup chopped dark chocolate (at least 70% cocoa)
- Sliced almonds for topping (optional)

Nutritional Information: (per serving) Calories: 280 | Total Fat: 20g | Carbohydrates: 20g | Fiber: 4g | Protein: 8g

Instructions:

1. Preheat your oven to 350°F (175°C). Coat a loaf pan with coconut oil or line it with parchment paper.
2. In a large mixing bowl, whisk together cocoa powder, almond flour, baking soda, baking powder, and salt.
3. In another bowl, whisk together honey or maple syrup, melted coconut oil, eggs, Greek yogurt, vanilla extract, and ground ginger until well combined.

4. Pour your wet ingredients into your dry ingredients and mix until well combined.

5. Gently fold in the chopped dark chocolate until it is evenly distributed throughout the batter.

6. Pour the batter into the prepared loaf pan, spreading it out evenly.

7. Sprinkle sliced almonds on top of the batter, if using.

8. Bake in your preheated oven for 55-60 minutes, or when an inserted (into the center) toothpick comes out clean.

9. Remove the pound cake from the oven and let it cool in the pan for 10-15 minutes before transferring it to a wire rack to cool completely.

10. Once cooled, slice the ginger chocolate pound cake and serve.

Serving Suggestions: Enjoy this moist and flavorful ginger chocolate pound cake as a delicious dessert or snack. Serve it with a dollop of Greek yogurt or whipped cream and fresh berries for a delightful treat. Alternatively, enjoy it alongside a cup of herbal tea or coffee for a cozy afternoon indulgence.

Almond Macaroons

- **Preparation Time:** 45 minutes
- **Serves:** 12 (2 macaroons per serving)
- **Size per Serving:** 2 macaroons

Ingredients:

- 2 cups almond flour
- 1/2 cup honey or maple syrup
- 2 large egg whites
- 1 teaspoon almond extract
- Pinch of salt
- Sliced almonds for garnish (optional)

Nutritional Information: (per serving) Calories: 160 | Total Fat: 10g | Carbohydrates: 15g | Fiber: 2g | Protein: 5g

Instructions:

1. Preheat your oven to 325°F (160°C). Line a baking sheet with parchment paper.
2. In a large mixing bowl, combine almond flour, honey or maple syrup, egg whites, almond extract, and a pinch of salt. Mix until a sticky dough forms.

3. Using a small cookie scoop or your hands, shape the dough into small balls and place them on the prepared baking sheet.

4. Press down slightly on each ball using the back of a spoon or your fingers to flatten them.

5. If desired, press a sliced almond into the center of each macaroon for garnish.

6. Bake in the preheated oven for 15-18 minutes, or until the macaroons are golden brown around the edges.

7. Remove from the oven and let the macaroons cool on the baking sheet for 5 minutes before transferring them to a wire rack to cool completely.

8. Once cooled, serve the almond macaroons and enjoy!

Serving Suggestions: These almond macaroons make a delightful gluten-free dessert or snack. Enjoy them with a cup of herbal tea or coffee for a cozy treat. Keep any remaining portions in an airtight container at room temperature for up to 3 days.

Wheat-Free Chip Cookies

- **Preparation Time:** 40 minutes
- **Serves:** 24 cookies
- **Size per Serving:** 1 cookie

Ingredients:

- 2 cups almond flour
- 1/2 teaspoon baking soda
- 1/4 teaspoon salt
- 1/4 cup coconut oil, melted
- 1/4 cup honey or maple syrup
- 1 large egg
- 1 teaspoon vanilla extract
- 1/2 cup dark chocolate chips (at least 70% cocoa)

Nutritional Information: (per serving) Calories: 100 | Total Fat: 8g | Carbohydrates: 6g | Fiber: 1g | Protein: 2g

Instructions:

1. Preheat your oven to 350°F (175°C). Line a baking sheet with parchment paper.
2. In a large mixing bowl, whisk together almond flour, baking soda, and salt.

3. In another bowl, whisk together melted coconut oil, honey or maple syrup, egg, and vanilla extract until smooth.
4. Pour your wet ingredients into your dry ingredients and mix until smoothly combined.
5. Gently fold in dark chocolate chips until they are evenly distributed throughout the dough.
6. Using a cookie scoop or tablespoon, drop rounded tablespoons of dough onto the prepared baking sheet, spacing them about 2 inches apart.
7. Press down lightly on each cookie using the back of a spoon or your fingers to flatten them slightly.
8. Bake in the preheated oven for 10-12 minutes, or until the cookies are golden brown around the edges.
9. take the cookies out of the oven and allow them to cool on the baking sheet for 5 minutes before transferring them to a wire rack to cool completely.

10. Once cooled, serve the wheat-free chip cookies and enjoy!

Serving Suggestions: Enjoy these delicious wheat-free chip cookies as a satisfying dessert or snack. Serve them with a glass of almond milk or your favorite hot beverage for a delightful treat. Keep any leftover cookies in an airtight container at room temperature for up to 5 days.

Pineapple Jello

- **Preparation Time:** 4 hours 15 minutes (including chilling time)
- **Serves:** 6
- **Size per Serving:** 1/2 cup

Ingredients:

- 2 cups pineapple juice (unsweetened)
- 2 tablespoons gelatin powder
- 1/4 cup honey or maple syrup (optional, adjust to taste)
- 1 cup diced fresh pineapple

Nutritional Information: (per serving) Calories: 60 | Total Fat: 0g | Carbohydrates: 15g | Fiber: 0g | Protein: 1g

Instructions:

1. Pour 1/2 cup of pineapple juice into a small bowl. Sprinkle gelatin powder over the juice and let it sit for 5 minutes to bloom.

2. In a small saucepan, heat the remaining 1 1/2 cups of pineapple juice over medium heat until it starts to simmer.

3. Once simmering, remove the saucepan from heat and stir in the bloomed gelatin mixture until completely dissolved.

4. If using honey or maple syrup, stir it into the pineapple juice mixture until dissolved. Adjust sweetness to taste.

5. Allow the mixture to cool slightly before pouring it into individual serving glasses or a large serving dish.

6. Add diced fresh pineapple into the glasses or dish with the pineapple juice mixture.

7. Place the glasses or dish in the refrigerator to chill for at least 4 hours, or until the jello is set.

8. Once set, serve the pineapple jello chilled and enjoy!

Serving Suggestions: Serve this refreshing pineapple jello as a light and fruity dessert or snack. Garnish with additional diced pineapple or fresh mint leaves for extra flavor and presentation. You can also layer the jello with coconut cream or yogurt for a tropical twist. Cover any leftovers and store them in the refrigerator for up to 3 days.

Pumpkin Pie

- **Preparation Time:** 1 hour 30 minutes

- **Serves:** 8

- **Size per Serving:** 1 slice

Ingredients: *For the Crust:*

- 1 1/2 cups almond flour

- 1/4 cup coconut oil, melted

- 1 tablespoon honey or maple syrup

- 1/2 teaspoon ground cinnamon

- Pinch of salt

For the Filling:

- 1 can (15 ounces) pumpkin puree

- 3/4 cup coconut milk (full-fat)

- 1/2 cup honey or maple syrup

- 2 large eggs

- 1 teaspoon vanilla extract

- 1 teaspoon ground cinnamon

- 1/2 teaspoon ground ginger

- 1/4 teaspoon ground nutmeg

- Pinch of salt

Nutritional Information: (per serving) Calories: 300 | Total Fat: 20g | Carbohydrates: 25g | Fiber: 5g | Protein: 6g

Instructions:

1. Preheat your oven to 350°F (175°C). Coat a 9-inch pie dish with coconut oil.

2. In a medium bowl, mix together almond flour, melted coconut oil, honey or maple syrup, ground cinnamon, and a pinch of salt until a dough forms.

3. Press the dough evenly into the bottom and up the sides of the prepared pie dish.

4. In a large mixing bowl, whisk together pumpkin puree, coconut milk, honey or maple syrup, eggs, vanilla extract, ground cinnamon, ground ginger, ground nutmeg, and a pinch of salt until smooth.

5. Pour your pumpkin mixture into your prepared crust.

6. Put the pie dish on a baking sheet and place it in the preheated oven.

7. Bake for 52-60 minutes, or until your filling is set and you have a golden brown crust.

8. Take your pumpkin pie out of the oven and allow to cool completely on the wire rack.

9. Once cooled, slice the pumpkin pie and serve.

Serving Suggestions: Serve this delicious pumpkin pie as a festive dessert for special occasions or as a comforting treat during the fall season. Top each slice with a dollop of whipped coconut cream.

Beverages/Smoothies for Blood Type O

Rice Milk

- **Preparation Time:** 10 minutes
- **Serves:** 4
- **Size per Serving:** 1 cup

Ingredients:

- 1 cup cooked rice (white or brown)
- 4 cups water
- 1-2 tablespoons honey or maple syrup (optional)
- 1 teaspoon vanilla extract (optional)
- Pinch of salt

Nutritional Information: (per serving) Calories: 70 | Total Fat: 0g | Carbohydrates: 15g | Fiber: 0g | Protein: 1g

Instructions:

1. In a blender, combine cooked rice and water.
2. Blend on high speed for 1-2 minutes until the mixture is smooth and well combined.
3. Strain the mixture through a fine mesh sieve or cheesecloth into a large bowl or pitcher to remove any remaining rice grains.

4. If desired, sweeten the rice milk with honey or maple syrup to taste and add vanilla extract for flavor.

5. Stir in a pinch of salt for balance.

6. Transfer the rice milk to a glass bottle or jar and refrigerate until chilled.

7. Serve the rice milk cold and enjoy!

Serving Suggestions: Enjoy rice milk as a dairy-free alternative to cow's milk in your favorite beverages, cereals, or recipes. Use it as a base for smoothies, pour it over granola, or enjoy it on its own as a refreshing drink. Tweak the sweetness and flavorings to match your personal taste preferences. Keep the leftovers in your refrigerator for up to 4-5 days.

Walnut Milk

- **Preparation Time:** 10 minutes (plus soaking time)
- **Serves:** 4
- **Size per Serving:** 1 cup

Ingredients:

- 1 cup raw walnuts
- 4 cups water

- 1-2 tablespoons honey or maple syrup (optional)
- 1 teaspoon vanilla extract (optional)
- Pinch of salt

Nutritional Information: (per serving) Calories: 200 | Total Fat: 20g | Carbohydrates: 4g | Fiber: 2g | Protein: 4g

Instructions:

1. Place the raw walnuts in a bowl and cover them with water. Allow them to soak for nothing less than 4 hours or overnight.
2. After soaking, drain and rinse the walnuts under cold water.
3. In a blender, combine soaked walnuts and 4 cups of fresh water.
4. Blend on high speed for 2-4 mins until you have a smooth and creamy mixture.
5. Strain the walnut milk through a fine mesh sieve, nut milk bag, or cheesecloth into a large bowl or pitcher to remove any remaining walnut pulp.

6. If desired, sweeten the walnut milk with honey or maple syrup to taste and add vanilla extract for flavor.
7. Stir in a pinch of salt for balance.
8. Transfer the walnut milk to a glass bottle or jar and refrigerate until chilled.
9. Serve the walnut milk cold and enjoy!

Serving Suggestions: Use walnut milk as a creamy and nutty dairy-free alternative in your morning coffee, tea, or smoothies. Enjoy it over cereal, oats, or granola, or use it in baking and cooking recipes. Experiment with flavor variations by adding cocoa powder, cinnamon, or dates for a delicious twist. Keep the leftovers in your refrigerator for up to 4-5 days.

Pineapple Protein Shake

- **Preparation Time:** 5 minutes
- **Serves:** 1
- **Size per Serving:** 1 glass

Ingredients:

- 1 cup fresh or frozen pineapple chunks
- 1/2 cup plain Greek yogurt
- 1/2 cup unsweetened almond milk

- 1 scoop vanilla protein powder
- 1 tablespoon honey or maple syrup (optional)
- Ice cubes (if using fresh pineapple)

Nutritional Information: (per serving) Calories: 250 | Total Fat: 2g | Carbohydrates: 35g | Fiber: 3g | Protein: 25g

Instructions:

1. In a blender, combine pineapple chunks, plain Greek yogurt, unsweetened almond milk, vanilla protein powder, and honey or maple syrup (if using).

2. If using fresh pineapple and desire a colder shake, add a handful of ice cubes to the blender.

3. Blend all the ingredients on high speed for 1-2 minutes until smooth and creamy.

4. Sample the shake and, if needed, adjust the sweetness by adding more honey or maple syrup to your liking.

5. Pour the pineapple protein shake into a glass and serve immediately.

Serving Suggestions: Enjoy this refreshing pineapple protein shake as a nutritious breakfast or post-workout snack. Customize the shake by adding spinach or kale for extra greens, or toss in a handful of berries for added flavor and antioxidants. Garnish with a slice of pineapple or a sprinkle of shredded coconut for a tropical touch.

Lemonade

- **Preparation Time:** 10 minutes
- **Serves:** 4
- **Size per Serving:** 1 cup

Ingredients:

- 1 cup freshly squeezed lemon juice (about 4-6 lemons)
- 4 cups cold water
- 1/2 cup of maple syrup or honey(adjust to taste)
- Ice cubes
- Lemon slices for garnish (optional)
- Fresh mint leaves for garnish (optional)

Nutritional Information: (per serving) Calories: 80 | Total Fat: 0g | Carbohydrates: 22g | Fiber: 0g | Protein: 0g

Instructions:

1. In a large pitcher, combine freshly squeezed lemon juice, cold water, and honey or maple syrup.
2. Stir the mixture until the sweetener is completely dissolved.
3. Taste the lemonade and adjust sweetness if necessary by adding more honey or maple syrup.
4. Add ice cubes to the pitcher to chill the lemonade or fill individual glasses with ice.
5. Stir the lemonade again before serving to ensure the ingredients are well mixed.
6. If you like, garnish each glass with a slice of lemon and a sprig of fresh mint.
7. Serve the lemonade cold and enjoy!

Serving Suggestions: Serve this classic lemonade as a refreshing beverage on hot summer days or alongside your favorite meals. Pair it with grilled meats, salads, or sandwiches for a refreshing contrast. Customize the lemonade by adding sliced strawberries, raspberries, or cucumber for extra flavor and visual appeal. Cover any leftovers and store them in the refrigerator for up to 3 days.

Lime Slushie

- **Preparation Time:** 5 minutes
- **Serves:** 2
- **Size per Serving:** 1 glass

Ingredients:

- 2 cups ice cubes
- 1/2 cup freshly squeezed lime juice (about 4-6 limes)
- 1/4 cup maple syrup or honey (adjust to taste)
- 1/2 cup cold water
- Lime slices for garnish (optional)
- Fresh mint leaves for garnish (optional)

Nutritional Information: (per serving) Calories: 80 | Total Fat: 0g | Carbohydrates: 22g | Fiber: 0g | Protein: 0g

Instructions:

1. In a blender, combine ice cubes, freshly squeezed lime juice, honey or maple syrup, and cold water.
2. Blend on high speed for 1-2 minutes until the mixture is smooth and slushy.
3. Taste the slushie and adjust sweetness if necessary by adding more honey or maple syrup.
4. Pour the lime slushie into glasses.
5. If preferred, garnish each glass with a slice of lime and a sprig of fresh mint.
6. Serve the lime slushie immediately and enjoy!

Serving Suggestions: Serve this zesty lime slushie as a refreshing beverage on hot days or as a tangy accompaniment to spicy dishes. Pair it with grilled fish, tacos, or salads for a burst of citrus flavor. Customize the slushie by adding a splash of coconut water or a handful of fresh berries for extra sweetness and color. Experiment with different citrus fruits like lemon or orange for variation.

Chapter 3

30 Days Meal Plan Sample

Please note that the provided meal plan is a sample and should not be interpreted as a recommendation to consume all the listed recipes in a single day.

This meal plan aims to offer inspiration and guidance for healthy meal preparation. Feel free to customize this plan to suit your preferences and dietary requirements. Adjust portions and ingredients based on individual preferences and dietary needs.

Day 1:

- Breakfast: Kale Salad
- Lunch: Spinach Feta Rice
- Dinner: Black Bean Soup with Meat
- Dessert/Snack: Ginger Chocolate Pound Cake
- Beverage/Smoothie: Rice Milk

Day 2:

- Breakfast: Easy Salmon Pesto
- Lunch: Tofu with Sauteed Vegetables
- Dinner: Chicken Veggie Soup

- Dessert/Snack: Almond Macaroons
- Beverage/Smoothie: Walnut Milk

Day 3:

- Breakfast: Buckwheat Scandinavian Pancakes
- Lunch: Vegetarian Lasagna
- Dinner: Gluten-Free Pizza Crust
- Dessert/Snack: Wheat-Free Chip Cookies
- Beverage/Smoothie: Pineapple Protein Shake

Day 4:

- Breakfast: Poached Eggs & Sweet Potatoes
- Lunch: Curried Shrimp
- Dinner: Chinese Stir-Fry
- Dessert/Snack: Pineapple Jello
- Beverage/Smoothie: Lemonade

Day 5:

- Breakfast: Omelet with Diced Lamb and Bell Peppers
- Lunch: Lemon-Herb Roasted Chicken with Green Beans
- Dinner: Fried Oyster Mushroom Mash
- Dessert/Snack: Pumpkin Pie
- Beverage/Smoothie: Lime Slushie

Day 6:

- Breakfast: Sardine Patties
- Lunch: Gluten-Free Oven-Fried Cod
- Dinner: Quick Bean Casserole
- Dessert/Snack: Lemon-herb roasted Chicken with Green Beans
- Beverage/Smoothie: Rice Milk

Day 7:

- Breakfast: Roast Parsnips
- Lunch: Rose Sauce with Pasta
- Dinner: Creamy Tuna Broccoli Rice
- Dessert/Snack: Wheat-Free Chip Cookies
- Beverage/Smoothie: Walnut Milk

Day 8:

- Breakfast: Kale Salad
- Lunch: Spinach Feta Rice
- Dinner: Black Bean Soup with Meat
- Dessert/Snack: Almond Macaroons
- Beverage/Smoothie: Pineapple Protein Shake

Day 9:

- Breakfast: Easy Salmon Pesto
- Lunch: Tofu with Sauteed Vegetables
- Dinner: Chicken Veggie Soup
- Dessert/Snack: Pineapple Jello
- Beverage/Smoothie: Lemonade

Day 10:

- Breakfast: Buckwheat Scandinavian Pancakes
- Lunch: Vegetarian Lasagna
- Dinner: Gluten-Free Pizza Crust
- Dessert/Snack: Pumpkin Pie
- Beverage/Smoothie: Lime Slushie

Day 11:

- Breakfast: Poached Eggs & Sweet Potatoes
- Lunch: Curried Shrimp
- Dinner: Chinese Stir-Fry
- Dessert/Snack: Ginger Chocolate Pound Cake
- Beverage/Smoothie: Walnut Milk

Day 12:

- Breakfast: Omelet with Diced Lamb and Bell Peppers
- Lunch: Lemon-Herb Roasted Chicken with Green Beans
- Dinner: Fried Oyster Mushroom Mash
- Dessert/Snack: Wheat-Free Chip Cookies
- Beverage/Smoothie: Rice Milk

Day 13:

- Breakfast: Sardine Patties
- Lunch: Gluten-Free Oven-Fried Cod
- Dinner: Quick Bean Casserole
- Dessert/Snack: Almond Macaroons
- Beverage/Smoothie: Pineapple Protein Shake

Day 14:

- Breakfast: Roast Parsnips
- Lunch: Rose Sauce with Pasta
- Dinner: Creamy Tuna Broccoli Rice
- Dessert/Snack: Pineapple Jello
- Beverage/Smoothie: Lemonade

Day 15:

- Breakfast: Kale Salad
- Lunch: Spinach Feta Rice
- Dinner: Black Bean Soup with Meat
- Dessert/Snack: Pumpkin Pie
- Beverage/Smoothie: Lime Slushie

Day 16:

- Breakfast: Easy Salmon Pesto
- Lunch: Tofu with Sauteed Vegetables
- Dinner: Chicken Veggie Soup
- Dessert/Snack: Ginger Chocolate Pound Cake
- Beverage/Smoothie: Walnut Milk

Day 17:

- Breakfast: Buckwheat Scandinavian Pancakes
- Lunch: Vegetarian Lasagna
- Dinner: Gluten-Free Pizza Crust
- Dessert/Snack: Wheat-Free Chip Cookies
- Beverage/Smoothie: Pineapple Protein Shake

Day 18:

- Breakfast: Poached Eggs & Sweet Potatoes
- Lunch: Curried Shrimp
- Dinner: Chinese Stir-Fry
- Dessert/Snack: Almond Macaroons
- Beverage/Smoothie: Lemonade

Day 19:

- Breakfast: Omelet with Diced Lamb and Bell Peppers
- Lunch: Lemon-Herb Roasted Chicken with Green Beans
- Dinner: Fried Oyster Mushroom Mash
- Dessert/Snack: Pineapple Jello
- Beverage/Smoothie: Lime Slushie

Day 20:

- Breakfast: Sardine Patties
- Lunch: Gluten-Free Oven-Fried Cod
- Dinner: Quick Bean Casserole
- Dessert/Snack: Pumpkin Pie
- Beverage/Smoothie: Rice Milk

Day 21:

- Breakfast: Roast Parsnips
- Lunch: Rose Sauce with Pasta
- Dinner: Creamy Tuna Broccoli Rice
- Dessert/Snack: Wheat-Free Chip Cookies
- Beverage/Smoothie: Walnut Milk

Day 22:

- Breakfast: Kale Salad
- Lunch: Spinach Feta Rice
- Dinner: Black Bean Soup with Meat
- Dessert/Snack: Ginger Chocolate Pound Cake
- Beverage/Smoothie: Pineapple Protein Shake

Day 23:

- Breakfast: Easy Salmon Pesto
- Lunch: Tofu with Sauteed Vegetables
- Dinner: Chicken Veggie Soup
- Dessert/Snack: Almond Macaroons
- Beverage/Smoothie: Lemonade

Day 24:

- Breakfast: Buckwheat Scandinavian Pancakes
- Lunch: Vegetarian Lasagna

- Dinner: Gluten-Free Pizza Crust
- Dessert/Snack: Pineapple Jello
- Beverage/Smoothie: Lime Slushie

Day 25:

- Breakfast: Poached Eggs & Sweet Potatoes
- Lunch: Curried Shrimp
- Dinner: Chinese Stir-Fry
- Dessert/Snack: Pumpkin Pie
- Beverage/Smoothie: Rice Milk

Day 26:

- Breakfast: Omelet with Diced Lamb and Bell Peppers
- Lunch: Lemon-Herb Roasted Chicken with Green Beans
- Dinner: Fried Oyster Mushroom Mash
- Dessert/Snack: Wheat-Free Chip Cookies
- Beverage/Smoothie: Walnut Milk

Day 27:

- Breakfast: Sardine Patties
- Lunch: Gluten-Free Oven-Fried Cod
- Dinner: Quick Bean Casserole

- Dessert/Snack: Pineapple Jello
- Beverage/Smoothie: Pineapple Protein Shake

Day 28:
- Breakfast: Roast Parsnips
- Lunch: Rose Sauce with Pasta
- Dinner: Creamy Tuna Broccoli Rice
- Dessert/Snack: Ginger Chocolate Pound Cake
- Beverage/Smoothie: Lemonade

Day 29:
- Breakfast: Kale Salad
- Lunch: Spinach Feta Rice
- Dinner: Black Bean Soup with Meat
- Dessert/Snack: Almond Macaroons
- Beverage/Smoothie: Lime Slushie

Day 30:
- Breakfast: Easy Salmon Pesto
- Lunch: Tofu with Sauteed Vegetables
- Dinner: Chicken Veggie Soup
- Dessert/Snack: Wheat-Free Chip Cookies
- Beverage/Smoothie: Rice Milk

Chapter 4

Conclusion

With this cookbook, you now have all the tools and tasty recipes needed to seamlessly embrace the Blood Type O lifestyle. By aligning your diet with the foods intended for your unique biochemistry, you're taking a major step toward experiencing enhanced energy, better weight management, and reduced disease risk.

Perhaps most importantly, you've unlocked the secret to making healthy eating something you actually crave instead of dread. The delicious, soul-satisfying meals in this book prove that nourishing your body optimally doesn't require deprivation or blandness.

Each recipe was a story, a testament to the resilience and adaptability that comes with age. They were chosen to bring joy to your table and health to your life, crafted with the knowledge that every ingredient matters, just as every moment does. As you continue to explore these recipes, let them be a daily reminder that eating well is a form of self-respect and an act of love for your body.

Remember, this book isn't just a collection of recipes; it's a companion in your kitchen, a silent guest at your table, and a witness to the laughter and conversations that bloom over shared meals. It's a celebration of life, of the years that have passed, and of the many more to come, filled with the richness that only good food and good company can provide.

So, take these recipes, these words, and let them live in your kitchen, in your hands, and in your heart. May every meal you prepare be a step towards vitality, and may every bite be a taste of joy. Here's to your health, to your happiness, and to the many delicious moments ahead.

Bon appétit!

Made in the USA
Monee, IL
19 October 2024

68133461R00059